I0450106

Get What You Want in Life with a Positive Mental Attitude

Norris Thomas

*Our mission is to efficiently provide the world's finest, most comprehensive book publishing
service, enabling every author to experience success. To find out how to publish your
book, your way, and have it available worldwide, visit us online at www.trafford.com*

Trafford rev. 3/1/2010

 www.trafford.com

North America & international
toll-free: 1 888 232 4444 (USA & Canada)
phone: 250 383 6864 ♦ fax: 812 355 4082

Part I:

THE PRINCPLE

This is the beginning of what I have studied through life experience. Everything you will read is profoundly the result of my failures and also my accomplishments. I can only speak from what I know of my beliefs and stories in truth by the information I have accumulated over the years of my life.

In my brief life I have had the opportunity to witness these profound principles to be just. You must believe that the mind is your biggest challenge and that you must overcome the mind to achieve. Life can become what you want it to be only if you as a person can put yourself in the mind frame that you are the master of your own destiny. It has been said over the years that a man can be anything that he wants to be, but there has been little input on the fact that you must have that as a goal. With no direction you have nowhere to go, without any knowledge you have no room to grow, without the know how to implement these principles you will forever stand still. I believe that if you use these strategies in everyday life you truly can reach the top. It has been said that when applied in the manner in which will be described later in the text that all one can hope for can be achieved.

Let me talk about the mind, the mind is your greatest asset, and with it you can overcome anything in life. As I sit here this day May 11, 2009 I have embarked on this journey to reach out to all that is willing to listen. I know that with the right mental attitude you begin the first step in writing your ticket to success. Without that you place yourself dead last in the race to success. Now I can only speak from what I have been through and what I have seen with my own eyes, but isn't that funny everyone on this plant has seen these things as well. It only takes little vision to see beyond that what you cannot see with the naked eye. People it is right there; how bad do you want it, how bad do you want to succeed, what is your definite of purpose in life. Many self help books have come about, many tapes, and so on, but one thing that has not changed is the message. That one who takes control of one's mind is the creator of one's destiny. You must place yourself in the mind frame that you are in control. How you may ask, by selling yourself to yourself. You cannot display you to others in costume because in time it will call for you to remove costume and show face value of who are you to tell others that this can work. Even though it has been proven many do not believe. Fear is one reason many choose not to believe. The fear of change; the fear of commitment; the fear of the unknown are three bridges one must overcome, Me myself has had to face these challenges to overcome my belief that the world owed me and that it had nothing to do with me as a person and that I was not in any position to demand anything to which I had not contributed. First step is this, you must give to get which is one principle that I have grown to learn. Meaning you cannot get anything in life without giving something back for it. How does one expect to get something for nothing and how dare you even think to desire anything from which you have not given. Give and you get plan and simple. This quote from a dear friend has been instrumental in my quest to find the true keys to success. This which has given me reason to believe that you as a person has what it takes to achieve anything in life. Mind over matter, God given talent or for some, that universal power that you have been blessed with from birth. Keyword the mind, use it. How hard is that, Yeah I forgot you are hell bent on what you have been doing all your life. That doesn't make since seeing that all that you have done has not gotten you any closer to what you feel you are destine to do in life. Wait maybe you don't know what it is you really want to do in life, ok I get the picture. I have got to build from ground up like a house. I know houses this I know that one thing in building a house is that you have to have a foundation first. With success it comes in the form of a vision. You have to envision a thought that you can achieve. You can be what you want to be but you must also understand that you must first take the steps to get there and it starts with the mind. You must train the mind it is said to be your key to opening your sixth sense. Positive mental attitude is the key. You must live positive, think positive believe in you because you and only you has the power to change you. If there's something you have always wanted to do get started right now. Set goals for yourself go after those goals until you achieve them then set higher goals, to get the results you want you have to take action. The eyes can only see so far. You must go as far as the eyes can see, and when you get there and only then will you be able to see further. Write down your plan in a detailed statement feed it daily into your brain until it has been memorized. Read it once in the morning and then at night as many times as you may need to keep yourself going. You have to remind the brain that you have an objective that you want to achieve. Try not to be overwhelmed by the outer world and focus on your inter world. Did you know that your inter world creates you outer world and that what you think in the mind attracts what you see with the eyes, now what if it where possible that you can think about something so hard that it becomes reality. Ladies and gentleman it is possible but it is no stroll in the park. Look at athletes who are at the top of there career. They got there by determination the will to become the best they trained day in and day out. They set goals which for them may have went something to the order of I want to be the best at what they are doing and that I will set in my mind that I will train hard, learn everyday better techniques, will myself to become the best. They believed in themselves they put in 110% to gain these skills. I get tired of people saying that a child is born with a skill that makes them great. No a child is born with a mind and with the right information fed into that child he or she can be truly whatever that child wants to be. You don't have to have the smartest parents in the world, you don't have to be the richest person in the world all you have to have is a vision and the will power to overcome any challenges that you may face in your quest to be happy in life. This which brings me to a story about a boy, his dad said when the boy was born that his son was going to play basketball he'll be one of the greatest to ever play the sport. Mom said she did not want him to play ball because she wanted him to be a lawyer and she tried to groom him to be just that. Dad got the son into basketball early and the boy was pretty good mom stayed on him about his studies and he graduated top of his class got a basketball scholarship also an academic scholarship to any college in America. Dad said, son get in and show the coach that you need to start right away because he knew scouts where in the crowds and that if they just saw one game and his skills he'd go straight to the pros. Mom told the son major in law so you can become a lawyer and make great money. By this time the boy was at an age where he had his own goal in mind as far as the boy could remember he always wanted to be a veterinarian and went on to study just that. He liked playing ball and the thought of being a lawyer but that wasn't his goal that was there's. People you cannot make someone else do anything that is not set in their mind. Everyone has their own mind so use it don't let anyone influence you to do anything you don't want to. Set your own goals follow through with them and believe in you because you are your own worst enemy.

Before you can move forward you must first commit to the goals you want to achieve. I stress that the mind is that ultimate step that must be taken. Redirect the mind and a many doors will open unto you. Life is not complicated. It is only that when you allow it to be that way. Instead of looking at what's not going right in your life, start acknowledging the good you get in life. Stop complaining about a problem and start finding solutions to fix the problem. When you look at a problem in that manner then you submit to defeat. This is not where I want you to be trust that you can overcome you. Believe in yourself know that you are worth more than what you have become. It doesn't matter you race, age, or creed everybody has the ability to succeed. I talk too many and one thing I get is that many do not have the will power or they just don't have the support. Become your own support and remember what I said, you must believe in yourself first in order for others to believe in you. Don't worry about the world abroad because you cannot change the world if you have not changed you. Remember the world is what you make it and that you create your own destiny. Earlier this day I was talking to my youngest niece about this book. I talked to her about the mind and she stopped me and said Norris you are not saying any thing different than what people already know. Hum I thought she was right, but then I came back with something that made her think. I said that is true everybody knows this to be the keys to overcoming any challenge. But why is it that people don't act on that principle, and I thought because it was never explained to people sooner and everybody knows that when you get to a certain age you feel that you know everything. Bologna you are never too old to learn anything. One thing one must overcome is that you can never know too much and that there is always something that you have not yet learned. Do not think for any second that you know everything, no one is a know it all I have never seen it. Stop blaming the world for your troubles. You are the reason you think that way not anyone else. Change your thoughts and watch your surroundings change. Remember a positive mind reflects a positive reality. The mind, the mind, yes I said it the mind I cannot stress that enough come on people wake up. It has nothing to do with everyone else it is you. It is not the war, the economy, the housing market, the stock market, the government, your spouse, the dog, and on, and on, and on. Take responsibility for you and stop blaming everyone else, because you are the reason you are in your position no one else just you. My vision comes from something more powerful than anything on this plant the gift that you have been blessed with is your mind. My world has nothing to do with earthly possessions it revolves in between my two ears my mind. I control my level of success I am the master of my own destiny I believe in me I am stronger mentally and physically I have sound health I can do anything that I put my mind to. Say this over and over until you believe that you truly are the master of your own destiny. It's not that hard once you get started just stay focused and you will succeed this I know I have been there. Think that if what you have been doing is not working what is wrong with trying something different.

You must have a purpose that is your reason for being on this earth. Mind you that it is not to hold space. Laziness is a disease that can be cured, but only if you are willing to change your useless habits. Find inspiration get involved in something that has meaning. Remember you must give something back and if you start now when you don't have much it will make it easier for you to continue that when you get where you want to be. I started by helping in my own neighborhood it doesn't matter what you do just get out of that lazy stage. Create daily plans to fill in your down time with things that can help you move forward. I read books or look up information that I don't know that I feel can help me in my business. You have to have a reason to achieve in life. Year's back I made a promise to myself that I would make sure my son would never have to worry about not having a roof over his head and give him the opportunity to do anything he wants to do in life. I said it would come from real estate so when he was born I got started. In that quest I found a broad range of things I could do to keep that promise. Later it spawned from that one goal to being able to help thousands. That's my purpose in life to help to put my findings in the hands of you. And I have got to tell you I am addicted to helping. I went from my son's daycare to the high schools across my city and so on. As far as I can go to who ever wanted to listen. Find your purpose and follow your heart I promise you if it is true then you will not have any problem with achieving it. Trust you if you have directed your mind for achievement then you cannot go wrong. But if you have got the idea from the beginning which is the mind then your purpose will find you. Why you say because that is why you are here why else would you be here why would you want to be here? Without purpose you are a wasted space and the world is getting too crowded with people with no purpose. That's why it is easy to be successful we need more successful people we are thinning. Think if Thomas Edison did not work day and night on his theory that he could make light bulbs using electricity where we would be. I'm sure that in time someone may have came up with that but in that time that was phenomenal. Did you know he failed over thousands of times talk about the determination of one man; he did it though oh and get this he only had a few months of schooling his entire life. He put his mind to it and he succeeded so why can't you. It has nothing to do with the world around you it is you. Find your purpose and add to history don't become wasted space. Focus on your inter world and then your outer world will be created. Do these things even when you don't feel like it get out of that lazy stage. Follow your heart believe in you I cannot say that enough because it starts with you. You are here to get something done get it done find what it is and get started the world does not need another person sitting on there you know what and doing nothing. Yes it's easy to sit and do nothing but you know what you get when you do nothing a whole bunch of nothing. Why not make a difference why not help why not care about your life. Stop wasting your time face it you only have a set time on earth why not make it worth something. Leave your family with something they can use. If you have gifts use it.

Knowledge is power that statement is true but without the know how to direct that knowledge into purpose then all that you know means nothing. I tell you that you can never stop learning no matter how old you are it is always something that you don't know. You must in order to succeed surround yourself with positive influence. Seek out those that are skilled in the fields in which you know nothing about. Brand your goals in the minds of others in a manner in which they feel obligated to serve your purpose. You cannot know everything today but you always have tomorrow to learn more than what you knew yesterday. Henry Ford founds this out and with his little education he knew more about being a leader and surrounding himself with people that knew the things that he had not yet figured out. He got people to believe in his vision. If you have sold you to you then it will not be hard to sell you to others because they will believe in your goals. To some just being a part of something is golden for you it is the accomplishments of achievement. Don't be afraid to get an opinion from others because that opinion if positive maybe the key to unlocking your success. Share your information with others I can tell you this because I to have been there. I have gotten more information just by expressing my thoughts than me sitting still keeping my visions to myself. Know that you are one of a kind and that you hold the key to achievement and that you are willing to help others and people will follow suit. One thing I have learned is that the world is filled with many followers it's the leaders that we lack. Hint, it's more room for leaders than there is room for followers. Things don't get invented if everybody is waiting on them to be invented. Somebody has got to have a vision why not you. Trust you and your ability to align yourself with others that inspire you and model yourself after those that have succeeded before you. The law of nature does not change. What you do reflects what you see. History shows this like the saying you are what you eat you become what you think. All great men became great because they use the minds of those that knew what they had not yet gained. Your team must love what they do and be all into the outcomes good or bad. Once you get going the doors of the universe will open up to you, therefore creating you infinite goal. Another thing with that is this it's not what you know it's who you know. Simple and put gather you a winning team that is willing to go the extra mile to get the job done.

This brings me to your power team you must develop a power team. This is a group of people that will come together behind you to achieve your goals. Remember you can't possibly know everything at one time you must have people that know the things you don't know. You must have a strong mind state to get these people to rally behind you. If your idea is sound then that will not be a problem. In this day and time you have a flock of different businesses that offer their services to those with a definite plan. Inspiration is the key because for some of them their hope comes from you. Become the mastermind over seeing your team and leading your team and with the right group of people you will see your vision come to light. Do not think for a second that any one man in history has every made it to the top on his own. In some fashion others played a part in there move from the bottom to the top. May it be a vision they got to the very structure of their operation. You must be the best in order to get the best. You don't want to hire in those that do not support the message you are trying to send out. I remember working for a grocery store out of Memphis, TN by the name of Piggly Wiggly, as a manager I gave opportunities to a lot of people I felt needed a job at the time. I found that not all that apply are willing to go the extra mile some are just looking for payday. Those types will never mean your company any business. You must screen the people you are looking for to make sure you get the right person for the job. They have to be willing to do whatever it takes to get the job done and that is getting you closer to your goals. They have to have a passion for their part in helping you. Watch the company you keep because your business will reflect who you have working for you. Ask yourself do you know anything about the stock market. Do you know anything about building houses? You may know how to sell a house but have you ever built a house. Those are two different professions and though some know everything you still would have to call an inspector, laborers and so on you can't know everything that is why you must continue to learn and grow. Take this try everyday to learn something new. Find people that can help your business grow from knowing the things you don't know. Most people use the help of others to get things going for their company.

Remember you will always have to have somebody to help you. Don't be afraid to ask for help sometimes it's best to ask privately seeing that you may have people around you that look for you to fail. Those type of people will always have negative thoughts and that is something you don't need. If you can get rid of them get them out of your circle. If they are family which you will have at least one try not to associate with them as much. Keep you distance from all negative people remember they mean you no good and they will only bring you down. Circle yourself with positive people that know the things you don't know and learn from them you can not grow if everyone around you knows less than what you know. Focus on attracting the best possible people to keep you motivated and going towards your goal.

Believe in yourself first in order to have others believe in you. Have faith know that your dreams can come true. Build faith around your goals you will need it. It will ensure that you never lose hope and keep you motivated towards your goal. Faith can be acquired if the right positive mind state is there to help manifest it into action. Trust in the decisions you make and have faith that you are capable of making tough decisions wanting success will not get you any closer to your goals. You must believe you can succeed with full passion. You will never get success by having faith today and doubting tomorrow. Trust me it will be like for every step you take forward you will fall 10 steps back. Faith is instrumental in your mold for success you have to have faith in what you are doing because you have to believe in you. Faith starts with you it is in you and it doesn't have to be tied to any religion. Faith is the principle in which you believe in that which you stand for.

Who are you? What makes you different from everyone else? Why should people respect you? How can you achieve this persona? I'll tell you how by understanding that how you carry yourself will be the reflection to which people categorize you in the world. Have you every heard the saying you are what you eat. Well the same goes for how you treat others you must treat others in the same way you want to be treated. Develop a personality that is undeniable to others. You can change the way people view you in a way that can excel you to a more definite stance in the world. Look at Bill Gates; him and his wife have dedicated much of their success to their foundations. Rich people do give and they give a lot. I feel that in one part of you building a new persona you must fit the give factor in. how can you truly enjoy riches knowing that there may be a child that is in need. Simple and put either start a foundation or get involved with one. You cannot enjoy real riches if all you are doing is taking. Now the saying it is better to give than receive is up to you and how you translate it, but think if everybody gives and no one receives then what would be the use. Make enough to support you and to be able to give. Now think for a minute that does not mean that because you got it you should not receive somebody has to receive why not you if at the same time you are giving. Be thankful in receiving from others. Not saying that it would have to be in money but also knowledge, wisdom, respect, trust, and so on. Train yourself to be a people person, remember that you can never know who you may need until you need them. People will not respect you if you cannot respect them that which is universal with all. It can be hard for one to change that which they are a custom to but when you do you will open the doors to a whole new world. Feel good about you on the inside and the outside will manifest into what you feel. Everybody wants to be liked in some way but understand no one owes you anything so don't look for recognition just know that by being the best you can be that will draw good people around you. Learn to be humble and never look down on anyone if anything you should try helping lift people up. The world has become a world of if it doesn't benefit me, then screw everybody else. Thinking about yourself all the time will never get you anywhere. Learn to change negative energy into positive energy. When you are confronted with negative energy give off positive energy and watch the change. Positive emotions can eliminate negative emotions. You will soon find people will love to be around you and that they will go out of their way to help you. Here is something you can use. Instead of looking for someone to give you a hand, start giving a hand to others. When you help others in return others will help you. Do not look for approval except for the consciousness of doing your best. Meaning, don't look for a reward because you helped somebody do it because it's the right thing to do period. The universe will open a many doors unto you trust I know. Don't be afraid to be judged besides if you are a good person then the world will lay at your door step, and all you will need to do is step out on top of the world with pride.

I must take a break from the topic of the book to share with you true revelations to the principles I speak. Today was my test I was faced with adversity after adversity. It was like everything you could think to go wrong did go wrong. I won't get into detail but let's say today was not my day. Then I thought about what I have been talking about all this time and what this book is about. I mean how can I write about something tell others about these profound teachings and not lead by example. People this how easy it is to fall back into your old ways. You see when you are changing who you are it can be hard but it can be easier to fall back into your old ways. There are two types of people in the world those that just go with the flow and the ones that take action to change the flow. For the ones that take action it will feel as if the world is against you, but fear not that is the thing that separates the strong from the weak, the true from the fake. Remember the universe will not bend for any one that wants to be part time. Either you are all in or not at all period. Teams do not win by playing half the game. You can't run half the race and think that you will win first place. Unless you are the only one running you will never get there half way. Everyday will be a struggle but you have to stay strong do not let go of what you have been dreaming of. Don't continue to be a part of a statistic be your own person take control of you. Man was made for achievement we were made to succeed. To the ones that are content with going with the flow what can I say but things will never change for you. What's wrong with living a good life? Why would you not want vast riches I mean if it is out there for you to get why not get it. I'll tell you why you are lazy you think getting rich will come from a five dollar scratch off, sorry but that isn't going to happen, and even if it does for the one percent of the population that wins the lottery most never have it very long, they go back to their old ways broke. What I am telling you is just the opposite it will take hard work, you have to have a plan, you must stay focused. Everyday remind yourself of what your goal is and stick to it. In some cases a lot could be riding on you following through with your goal. It may be something that can help others you never know who could be affected. As long as you are reaching for something that is righteous then it may be a benefit for others as well. That should make you want to achieve knowing that it may help someone else. Here's a thought think about what you can do to help others and work on that. Remember you can get what you want if you just help enough other people get what they want.

Now that we are back on focus let's talk about what we can do to get ahead even in your current situation try and think for a minute how much of you do you think you devote to the job you do. Most would say you give it your all. Seriously how much do you actually think you put into your job? Try only 25 percent that's a small number I know right but it is true. You only put 25 percent of your all into what you do. How about if I let you in on a secrete I feel I can tell you right off and it won't affect anything unless you implement all the strategies I talk about. It has been said that the world takes its hat off to those that put 50 percent into what they do and opens the gate to any personal achievement you seek if you put 100 percent into what you do. Meaning don't look at your job as a way to pay the bills or because that's all you can find. If that's the case get out now and start doing what you love. Don't work hard for the money work because you like your job and it makes you feel good about going. I remember working for a grocery store in Memphis, TN when I was young I always wanted to work for this store and year after year I was turned down. Finally some years later I got that job and because I love that job I worked under some messed up conditions at times.

I remember working as a department head making 7.35 an hour part-time with no benefits. When at other stores the same person doing the same thing I was doing make a heck of a lot more than me was full-time and had benefits as well. People use to ask me how I could even do it. For me it wasn't about the money I loved my job I came in everyday ready to get the job done I really, really loved my job and I was good at it to. Then one day my time came I had been working for about 2 years at a slow rate and then out of nowhere everything changed. I got an offer to run the grocery department in a new store that was to open I said yes before I could change my mind my pay changed. I was making more money and my job got a whole lot easier. I never worried about the recognition of doing my best I just came in and did my best because that's what I loved to do. In life sometimes you have to go the extra mile just because you never know who is watching. On day while at work a lady came up to me that I had never seen before she said she liked my work ethic and offered me a job making a lot of money plus bonuses. I turned her down why because it wasn't about the money I found something I liked and stuck to it about a week later I got a raise and was in line to receive bonuses way more than what she offered me. I suggest that if you want to get ahead in your job find something you are good at and stick to it period. No man walks into a job with the skills of greatness it is accomplished by time and effort. You get better with time but if that's where you see yourself and it makes you feel good go get it. Think about it if you are not in motion on something then nothing will ever happen you will sit still. Formulate a sound plan and put it into action, your future depends on it. And the longer you wait the longer it will be before you achieve your goals. Love the job you do and don't worry about the money because with good work ethic comes more riches to you than you may ever imagine. I must say to you I have been there so I can say that these principles do work. Then you will always have the negative people in your head saying you can't and why would you want to do that. Block them out of your head work hard for now to let your money work hard for you later. That's what rich people do they cut back now save and invest work hard then set up passive income wealth with their investments. Now they don't have to work hard their money works hard for them. Don't place your attention on what you are paid focus on what you can offer them and work at that a good company will notice their assets and begin to compensate you according to your worth. If your work is worth 10,000 dollar a year then that's probably what you will make. You can't get caught up in what you make right now because that isn't what you will be worth later. You can take what you make now invest what you can save where you can and still live ok. That's how the rich get rich then you'll wake up and won't have to go to work.

People you have to want to do it for yourself first before you can ever move forward in life. What do you really want in life make it a burning desire within your mind, body, and soul I mean you got to feel it and you have to believe in you, know that you can do anything you want in life? You are the master of your own destiny and you must control that destiny. Initiate yourself let your goals be the fire you need to keep going. Trust that you know what you want now let's get it. Think as if you have no time to waste so you have got to get it because the world is passing you by and you are on the road to catch up. Why are there a lot of poor people and not many rich people? I will tell you people are content with no let me change that people don't want to do the work it may take to get there and they have no personal initiative. We got to do better train your children to want everything in life to live a good secure life happy from poverty and oppression. Inside not outside we all know money can't buy happiness but when you feel good inside you move closer to physical riches. Want it for yourself why not I been telling you that you can think so hard that the universe will open up for you and you can get whatever you want in life. Have faith in your ability to achieve anything because boundaries can be broken if you break out of your old thinking ways. Feed yourself with positive thoughts and go hard on what you believe. You control what you think about so why not think about positive things why not live and act positive in spite of your circumstance. Yes it can be hard but it's worth it in the end. The road of life starts with you, make it what you want it to be and stay true to yourself. Don't worry about what others may think, this is your life live it and in the process get rich. Start to control the mind and what you think about and watch your life change for the better. It's up to you to change the direction your life is going. Give yourself a head start with positive input from yourself. Be happy with you on the inside and the rest will fall in place.

With all that being said let's get down to the nuts and bolts. Now that you know the things you can do to totally change your life for the better let's put it into action. First you have to be discipline with these principles or it will not work. The result will vary so just because this book may take one person one way it may take you in another direction. Use these principles in everyday situations no matter the outcome if you have good sound ideas for your life then you will not be dissatisfied . Stick to the game plan because you can't go anywhere if you do not know where you are going. So your goals must be your outline to follow, carefully put your goals in order and stay on track. You will have a many obstacles that may present themselves but remember that it is just your imagination running wild and that you may need to adjust your thoughts to reflect your objective. Find a focal point to follow. Your goals should be easy to achieve don't set goals you know you cannot achieve. Set small goals that move you forward to your main objective and in time you will see yourself moving closer and closer to your dreams. The world is filled with distractions but if you control your own mind then the outside world will not affect you because you will be in another atmosphere mentally. You will get the results of what you think. No one has got far without having set goals. Look at your life can you see that because of how you carry yourself is the exact result for what you have and how your life has been. You have to lead by example in order for people to truly respect who you are and what you are trying to do. The mind can get out of hand but the step is to maintain control. You do this by meditation and focus careful planning and organized goals. At first it may seem hard to do but with repetition you will find that it will almost become natural to you. You will begin to harness your subconscious mind and manifest your deepest thoughts. Restrict your mind from anything that does not promote your growth. This is the first stage you must achieve in order to move toward your goals. This principle can be used in any situation just adjust and take what you need from it. Let meditation become a daily thing for you set aside time to sit in silence and reach your deepest thoughts. Remember in order to remain focused you must remind the mind of what you want. With so many distractions that you may face daily you must train the mind to hold steady to maintain what you believe in and that you control your own affairs.

Once you have got the understanding that you can control your mind you must control your attention. Some people tend to have what they would call short attention spans. Why is that you may ask because we have yet to take full control of our own mind. We know what we want but not knowingly we suppress our mind from the growth and development of what we want. That is why many people never start on that project that they had been dreaming of long ago. We tend to find excuses for why we cannot instead of using our mind to find solutions to the problems we face. If you use your mind to make excuses it will never have time to find solutions period. Make it your business to be attentive to solutions and you will find that no matter what the problem there is always a solution. "For every problem there is a solution". Look at it this way for every math problem there has to be an answer so for everything that you may go through it has to have a solution to change the outcome it a universal law what goes up must come down what's under the ground creates what's above the ground. When you can keep your attention focused on your goals you will find that any and everything you could think of can become a reality. It is my belief that with meditation you can train your mind to focus on something so hard that it can go from a simple thought to physical matter. Once you can keep your attention on something until it becomes desire you will see your dreams come true.

Third thing is that you need to get excited about what you are doing. Feel good about it and let the world know I mean if it makes you feel good who's to say that it can't help anyone else. What if you have a life saving invention or idea that that could save thousands do you think it would be of any benefit if you keep it to yourself no. So don't be selfish share you expertise with the world. Believe in what you have to offer and know that if you truly believe in it then others will as well. I have helped many, most not even directly, but maybe they got something out of what I have said. I talk to a lot of people I try to expand my belief to everyone I come across. I believe in my principles because they have worked for me and thousands of other people just like you. You truly have the power to change your outcome period. Sometimes I get so excited that I feel as if I were walking on clouds I want to tell as many people as I can. I have seen so much heart ache and then I have seen these principles in action change any failures and any disbelief literally right before my eyes. So go out work yourself up to the point that you don't see obstacles any more let the world know. When you believe in what you are doing and live through what you believe people will see and they will see you glow. Now if you are not excited to let the world know about what you are doing then maybe you are not ready. If you cannot get yourself excited then what you think you want may not be what you really want. Sounds fair to say I mean if you are not excited about it what makes you think someone else will be excited. Let's start by getting yourself use to getting excited I want you to stand in front of a mirror and go all out about your vision or idea just let yourself go right now it's just you in the room. Scream out loud "I believe in me" "I believe in what I have to offer" "I am so excited about my ideas and I must let the world know" repeat this over and over until you truly believe then go out and share it with the world by putting your plans into action. Remember there is somebody out there that needs your help. Become your own spokesperson promote yourself I mean why wouldn't you. Hello whose side are you on success's side or failure the choice is yours but you must choose. You cannot jump side to side or walk on the line. It is now or never the ball is in your court now that you know what you can do to make a difference in your situation. I'm telling you these principles will work in any situation whether it is to get a promotion, love, and marriage anything if you want it so badly that you can almost taste it go get it. Don't let anyone deter you from your objective. Go out and let the world know, this is your future what are you going to do about it.

I remember when it came to my job I use to get so excited about it that you would not catch me talking about anything else. I really loved my job. I would have people all the time tell me I was a little over board when it came to my job. To them my job was not important but for me it was the chance of a life time. Granted in the beginning it wasn't about securing a good long term job but over time that is exactly what it became. Daily my passion for my job grew it took me places I would have never thought I would go within that field. You see this is what I mean about getting excited about everything you do. At times I was so excited that it went from me getting the job for one reason to keeping the job for many other reasons. That my friend is what I call the fire deep inside you that no matter what you are into will in time make itself known. You see I always had a burning desire to succeed and the fact that I loved my job gave me a focal point to hold on to and that gave birth to my inner strength to evolve around my environment. So no matter what you are going through you can still give birth to that one thing that will make you great in anything you try. So get excited and tell the world put your ideas out there and if you believe in them truthfully I guarantee you will get what you are looking for.

Once you have mastered the first steps and have in control the mind and focused on what you want let your mind go to work. The imagination is a wild thing and can spawn a many things that can benefit you or lead you into destruction. But the good thing about that is that if you have control you will know when the mind is off track. Let your imagination fly it will be the base of all things that beginning. You have to imagine something before it can become physical it has to be a thought in order for it to become a reality. I'm not talking about a day dream the thing that I am talking about is pure and inside you. It does not care what you are going through it will show no matter what. This is why it is important that you master the first steps. The mind is all power and if directed in the wrong direction it can upset the balance in your life. That is why I say once you have it in your mind that you want the knowledge you must be ready to hold that knowledge. Once you can focus on one thing the imagination will roar like a lion it is human nature for the mind to think to evolve to create to challenge anything that ends with why and if you want the answers then you better start with control of the mind then let your imagination go and trust you will find the answers. What made Edison think to invent the light bulb what made man think to harness fire sail the seas fly as the birds do I will tell you and I'm afraid you already know the answer to that the imagination period. Open your mind and let it go if you need answers focus on the question at hand then let your imagination do its job and that is to think and find all the answers. I want you to sit and think about what goes into a lot of the things that man has invented over the years. Take an airplane for instance form all the components that went into the building of one to the theory that man used to make it fly through the air. Now tell me that the imagination is not amazing. You see when you have an idea that needs to be manifested that is when the imagination goes to work. This is what it was made to do I would hope you didn't think that the answers just fall from the sky into your brain. Your imagination is working 24 hours a day but it is up to you to direct your imagination on what you would like to accomplish. This is big the imagination is a major component in the steps to achievement.

In life you will have some defeat I always say that defeat depends on you. You must learn from your failures if not you put yourself in place to repeat the same mistake over and over again. No one is perfect so don't beat yourself up when you are faced with failure just learn from it and keep going. When you fail at something then that means that you have given up and you lose. Winners never give up they keep going until they succeed. I have seen people become a victim to defeat and that attitude embeds its self into their subconscious mind and everything they try they fail. Why because they had failure in their mind from the start so they fail before they begin. A man that fails to plan is a man that plans to fail. If you have a solid plan then you can use that as your outline and at times you may need to adjust your plans to meet with failure. Just keep going and do not give up failure is only failure when you let it stop you. Look at it this way demand of yourself to push through defeat and learn from it. This is your dream are you going to let defeat stop you. If so then you will never succeed period. You will have people to put you down as well and that can hold you back to so stay away from those that have nothing good to say about you. I tell people all the time if you have nothing good to say to me just say "oh that's good" and walk away. Do not entertain negative influence it is contagious and it will bring you down. Think of yourself as a winner in your race you can't lose because you are racing against yourself let yourself win for a change stop being a loser. It has nothing to do with anyone else it's up to you to learn form your failures and move past them. You have to be your own motivator your own cheer squad and cheer yourself to victory. You will make some mistakes everybody makes mistakes but for some that is where it ends and for others they learn from them and push forward. So don't be afraid to fail think of failure as a learning experience. If you are afraid to fail then guess what you will fail. Why you may ask because you will draw failure by think about failing. You will be thinking about failure so much that all you will create is failure. So you can not worry about failing just learn from it when you do.

Have you ever heard the saying time is money and money is time? You get paid for your time well what about making your money work for you without being on your time. You see money can be made without you even working for it through investing. There is nothing wrong with investing your money in the stock market as long as you do it smart. Budget your money and invest it to make money for you. Use your time to find other things that can move you forward in personal happiness. When you create a simpler life you will see a lot of the burden some people go through in life lifted off your shoulders. Get a grip on your life and stop creating the problems you face. Enjoy life by controlling how you live your life and use your time wisely. Once you learn to budget your time and energy then you will see life become much easier for you. If you wish to have riches you have to start changing how you spend your money. Most poor people are poor because they spend money that they don't have meaning they spend more in a pay period than they make in income. You have to start to spend less and save more. Most relationships end because of money you have to change your old habits in order to get ahead. Once you train your mind to spend responsibly then you will see your bank account grow. Half the things people buy they don't need so why do we buy them. I will tell you because we feel that it will fill that empty hole we have inside of us, but after that we still feel empty. So we never get anywhere and we stay in the same place as we started period. You can get control of this by watching what you spend. Sit down and write out your needs and your want then go from there. You will see that your wants the things you don't really need will outweigh your needs. Eliminate your wants and focus on your needs and watch your bank account grow.

Next you must have a clear and positive mental attitude. P.M.A. is the key to success in anything you do. Start looking at the good in life over the bad there's a good guarantee that the good always outweighs the bad. This will take deep meditation to learn to block out anything that is negative. Take time out of your day to meditate strictly on positive thinking. Once you have gained a true positive mental attitude then you will see that your life will become easier. You will find that things will start to work out for you. Other people will say you are just lucky but inside you and I know that luck didn't have anything to do with it. Positive thinking brings a positive and for filled life. This is a big principle to follow because without it your mind will be challenged daily by the negative influences of the world. I have told you that your mind is your center and that you feed your mind with every thought you think so why not think positive. It will clear your head and you will see adversity before it comes and you will be able to counter it and move forward. If you have mastered the things you have already read you will understand that with a positive mental attitude you lay down any road blocks you may face and if they do come you will be equipped to break through them. Positive thinking has the power to reverse any obstacles.

A while back my son's mother was going through some things in her life. It was like every time she tried to move forward she would get pushed back 5 steps. Everything was going wrong for her so she developed a negative mentality for everything she came across. By her having such a negative attitude for the things that were not going right she soon was losing on the positive things in her life because she focused so hard on the bad. I sat here down one day and we began redirecting her thoughts to positive things. I would tell her when she finds herself faced with defeat to immediately focus on the positive. Instead of waking up and saying I don't know how I'm going to be able to do this say today I am going to do this no matter what it takes because I have to. She stopped flipping out when a job said no and kept going forward. She began to think positive about her life. I talked with her on a Monday by Wednesday she had found a job. Before that she had went almost two months looking for a job but she never got one because of her destructive thinking. Now she had all the qualifications for the jobs she was applying for she just had so much frustration that she was defeated before she every got started. That is what I am telling you if you have negative thinking then you defeat yourself before you ever get started period. That Wednesday she had gotten the job she never went on a interview for the job she applied for she talked then with the HR over the phone and the lady told her to work that Friday. She told her that in the beginning it wouldn't be many hours but instead of her getting herself down she accepted the job even though she was looking for something full time. That Saturday the lady called her and told her that she could take the case on full time so now she is working full time in that job. You see when you think positive over any adversity then anything that comes your way in a negative form will be dissolved by your strong positive mental attitude. You truly can change the outcome of life with positive thinking. Like the saying you are what you eat well you are also what you think so I suggest you think positive and watch your life change for the better. Try it why not we see that negative thinking doesn't work. Exercise your P.M.A.

Now with all that being said one thing you must have as well is good judgment in the decisions you make. You can't go out talking about things you know nothing about. You can't go out and get a job you have no qualifications for it just doesn't work that way. I believe you should trust your decisions but make sure that they are accurate to fit whatever you are deciding on. If you are making bad choices you will get bad results period. So make sure you think about things first then make your decision. Would you put your money in a bank that is going out of business no, or would you? When it comes to a lot of businesses they fail because of some of the choices that are made. They simply make bad decisions because they have not thought out the best possible solutions to the problem. Make sure if you are making any choices you know what you are talking about. This is the time to be precise because your thoughts can make or break you. In any business venture you must know about it and if you plan on being successful then I suggest you learn as much as you can before you start. I don't think second guessing yourself is bad it only tells you that there may be something you are missing, because if you knew from the start there would not be any reason to second guess. Educate yourself in the field you are attempting that way you will be able to counter any problems that may come about.

When your life is balanced you will be able to have sound physical health. Take care of your body as well as your mind because the mind and body are connected and if your health is poor then you probably have poor thinking. Some illnesses come from the way you think. Depression can cause many illnesses so maintain your thoughts of good health. Exercise regularly it will give you energy and help to keep the mind focused when it is needed. Health is very important you have to be at your best to endure the challenges life may bring. Yoga can help with meditation which is needed for focus. I wouldn't say you would need to sign up for yoga classes a simple instructional video may suit you in the comfort of your own home or office. Set aside time out your day to focus on your health I cannot stress this enough good physical health is something that you will need period. You want to focus on prosperity not whether you are healthy or not. This theory may have different effects on some but for me I stopped worrying about aches and pains and without the help of medicine and doctors I have been able to mentally cure myself from lots of things. I'm not saying that you should stop going to the doctor or taking certain medicines I'm just saying don't just rely on some doctor or meds to cure you. The body was made to heal it's self so I'm sure your thinking has a lot to do with the healing process. I have seen some cancer patients overcome the illness while others of the same illness that got the same treatments and medical attention fall to the disease. Why is that they say that the meds may not help everyone but why. There has to be an answer to that. I believe it is in the thinking. Many go in and the doctors say they are to fare gone and that would make a person lose hope. Even though there have been people that where far gone that have survived. I believe the message should be changed to yes you are far gone but there is hope if you believe that you can make it there may be a chance that you can survive. Why shoot a person down before they even get started. Give yourself hope if no one else will tell yourself that sickness is a mind thing that you can overcome if you believe. Some hope is better than none at all so maintain your health mentally.

In life I believe you must be able to coexist with others. You are not the only human on earth so being able to get along with others is the key for you to be able to climb the ladder of life. It may even help you to associate with people with the same common interest as you. You want to be in an environment that highlights your talents. Working with people that comment your style is good and will make it easier for you to get along with others. You have to be able to get along with others in the work force because these are the people that will either work to help you or make your job hell. I'm not saying you should suck up to your co-workers for them to like you just treat them the way in which you would like to be treated. I was a manager for three years and the way I went about it to get others to like working for me was that I gave them the chance to show me what they could do. My theory was that if we tell you what you need to do and how to do it you don't need someone telling you daily what you are not doing right. Instead of drilling employees on what they weren't doing right I focused on what they were doing right. And in the same process worked with them on what they didn't get the first time. I used the good things to build their confidence until they got the things they didn't know. Most of them went on within a short period of time to being some of the best employees anyone could ask for others didn't get it because they really didn't care from the beginning so those few would end up quitting. I work with my employees to show them I'm not your typical boss I would get down and work with them. How can you ask someone to work for you and respect you if you don't even know what go into what they do. Now I can admit that the fact that I'm working with them I know what they should be capable of doing and if I'm working hard you should be working just as hard.

Everything that you have read prepares you for this last of principles your sixth sense this has nothing to do with you at all this is nature at its best the uncontrollable the reason trees grow the reason we age and the unexplained. Your sixth sense is your connecting force between you and the universe. If you have mastered the readings then this force has started working it states that what you think and draw comes into manifestation. It is not luck that got you where you are it is your purest thoughts and beliefs that have manifested into what you see. No man can stop nature and this is nature to the fullest. This is that cosmic force that you hold inside of you. I tell you that you can truly change the outcome of any uncertainty if you apply the principles I have stated. Mined you this is no easy task it takes practice and determination but I am certain that if you follow these principles that you will change the outcome of your life. I can truthfully say this because I have used them myself. Your sixth sense will kick in without you even knowing and you will see for yourself. Remember with this power comes great responsibility and you must be ready mentally to handle the power of controlling your own destiny rather than letting life just deal you straight out of the deck of old and battered cards of life. Take this knowledge and use it I can assure you that you will like the results you get. Take control of your life and live happy.

Part II:

WISE WORDS TO LIVE BY

You must be able to motivate yourself in order for you to achieve the things you want in life. Motivation is the key if you want something then go after it. If that is what you want then you should have no problem getting what you want. Be your own motivator. If you are not able to motivate yourself then you must be content with your status in life. Obviously you want more out of life so let that be your motivation to and get it done. You can have some of the best talents in the world but if you cannot motivate yourself then you will stand still. Take me for example I am what some would call a jack of all trades. I wanted to know how to do a lot of things so I learned. Now I know I can't do everything at once but at times I try. I love to learn about the things I don't know about. But that doesn't mean that I do everything that I know and the fact that I know how to paint cars does not mean I motivate myself to paint cars. I mean I'm good at it but I don't get up every day ready to paint cars. Some people know of this talent that I have but there are some people that don't know I have this talent and because I don't display this talent many will never know about it.

Everyday will be a test for you if you can not maintain your self motivation. At times it will seem as though the world is against you but you must stay focused. There are things you will face that may not go as you may plan but the real test is how you handle that pressure. Some crumble under the pressure of failure others learn from it and overcome it which one do you see yourself as. Remember winners never quit and quitters never win. Take this as a dose of motivation and apply it everyday. Turn yourself into a winner by adapting a winner's mentality and never under any circumstance give up on any thing you truly believe in. Learn from your mistakes and push ahead knowing that in the end the victory you are looking to receive will be great. In life I have faced great pressures but my will and determination always prevails over the short comings in life. Defeat is only defeat when you accept it as such and one will never be defeated if one pushes forward to victory. Know that you can overcome any challenges that you may face in life and keep yourself motivated. Use your failures as learning experience and try not to make them again. The more you push on the closer you will get to your goal. Failure can get you down believe me I know but it is up to you to decide whether or not you are going to let that defeat you or not. Zero in on your strengths and use them to overpower your weaknesses. If you allow your weakness to be the dominate one then you will be faced with defeat every time. Learn to eliminate your weakness to accomplish anything in life. This will take daily motivation in order to keep the mind trained and focused. Remember you control your end results and it is up to you to decide whether or not you fail or succeed period. In anything you do if you believe in it you must not by any means give up because failure becomes failure when you allow it to be failure. Turn failure into learning experience and push forward.

Stop looking for someone to say "hey there good job". Concentrate on just doing your best and opportunity will come. Don't choose a job just to be recognized do it because you love it. I worked two years at my job before it every paid off in my favor. One thing I learned was that while everybody else was talking about what they weren't getting I was more focused on the job that I loved to do. In those two years I worked hard and at times was severely under paid but that never bothered me why because I loved what I was doing. One day time came when there was such an opening available and I went for it. Because of my work ethnic there was no problem with me taking on that obligation I was ready and determined to be the best.

Today was a test of my strengths once again. You see every day is a test and once you take that step to change what is then you face the obligation to yourself to pull through and overcome the negatives that may arise. Love what you do if you choose to do anything first and for most period. Have a purpose and for fill that purpose. Remember that you have already set the bar for yourself now you must fall through with that. Trust that if you truly believe in your ability then you will not fell. I have always said that life is what you make it why not make it in your favor. Everybody will not agree to what you think of yourself so you must have an understanding of that and be able to live with that fact. Like I said do it for yourself. I hear of other books that tell you, you can be this and be that but truth be told you have to want it for yourself before it will ever manifest. Don't worry about if someone will notice what you are doing and just do it. When you want someone to notice you they never do until you mess up so just keep doing your best and live life the way you want. In the past I would always beat myself up about the fact that I never got what I felt that I deserved and that everybody owed me. But the truth to that was that it was never up to me to demand that anyone state my credit, and if they did who would it be for not them and not to help me per say but to give to myself that satisfaction. To me I am the best to you, you are the best but who's to say what is the best. Unless you control your outcome then what you think does not matter. Once you decide that you are in control of your destiny then and only then will you get the solutions that you seek in your quest to for fill you destiny. You have to understand that no one on this earth owes you anything and that if you want something then you have to get out there and get it period. In this day and time the race card does not mean the color of your skin the race is for those that choose to get out there and put forth the effort to be the best period. Once you change you and your life style only then will your life become whole or close to what you aspire it to be. But understand that there are no more people watching what you do than you yourself. You can become your biggest critic. You must take control and rise above any and all things that may have stopped you in the beginning. Believe that you are the best of the best and trust that in time you will see that you truly are the best and that you have survived the out skirts and moved towards you ultimate goal.

To some the thought that you should compromise shows a sign of weakness. That is by all means false. Some situations should be compromised for the greater good. Do not feed into that statement that to compromise shows that you are weak it is nothing of the sort. To compromise means that an agreement between two or more people have been simply adjusted to meet the needs of that particular party, and that of the group they have reached a solution to serve all within the situation. All things can be compromised but I feel it is safe to say that you have to know when to compromise. Do not cheat yourself but at the same time never should you be out there to cheat others. Let all parties win and in the end you will win more. Being able to compromise will put you in a position to control the results and some time people play hardball because they feel as thou you may be trying to get over on them. No one likes to be had so why try to screw them learn to compromise and you may see a lot of the time that things will fall in your favor. Be truthful to yourself and treat people with the respect they deserve, and work your problems out to benefit all that is involved. Understand that there is nothing weak about being the bigger man or woman. You get close to what you want and others get closer to what they want and everybody can be happy. But you have to stand down and be the bigger person.

In a lot of situations this can be used on the job, in the home, in anything that you may face. Know that to compromise gives you the upper hand in negotiations and if you suggest it first then chances are you will come out on top in the long run. That goes back to what I was saying earlier give and you get period. I myself truly believe in this theory because I have seen its affects and at times it will almost seem like a miracle has been performed but you will know that it really isn't it is merely the fact that you where able to handle the situation in a way that benefits all that are involved. It is good business to be flexible in doing business to insure that everyone that you do business with will know that you are fair and reasonable and willing to compromise to make sure everyone wins. Now I'm not saying that every deal in business must be compromise because at times you will come across people that are out to gain by tearing the next person down so that is something that you will have to judge for yourself. I am only saying that you should not have a closed mind about adjusting your wants to help close on any dealings in life.

In relationships it is ok to agree with your partner on things especially if it will affect the both of you. There has to be communication between the both of you so that you know the needs of each other and so you can come together and fulfill the wants of each involved. If your mate has an idea hear them out before you shot them down; what is the harm in that. It is 2009 not the year of the Neanderthal learn to reason with your mate and watch as your relationship grow. If you truly love that person then you should have no problem compromising with them. Learn to work through your problems with the laws of compromising and you will see a change I can assure you in that, but it has to go both ways. Building a strong relationship with people is not a one way street.

In almost everything you do you will always face competition there is always someone out there ready to do it better than you. Understand that law holds true in that in the end the strongest and the fittest will always be better than there competition. You want to aim for being the best and learn from your peers to better yourself. Competition is like a blue print to follow you learn what does not work and perfect them you learn what does work and apply them study those around you and pick up on their short comings to better you as a whole. Plain and put how else would you learn what not to do remember that if you don't have to go through it but you can gain from it then why would you cheat yourself by not using it to learn from it. Make life easier on you by studying what to do and what not to do. So many people go through life trying to do everything on their own. Stop wasting your time and put yourself ahead of the game by understanding that the game will never change it is the methods in how you reach a goal that will. Thomas Edison failed thousands of times do you think the next person after him that came in an redesign the light bulb started where he started no they took what he had already did and perfected it. In anything you do there is always someone that may have came before you with the idea that inspired you all you will do is build on it. Know that competition is good for everyone involved because it sets the bar of achievement for each individual to want to be the best in what they are doing.

Sometimes you can even compete with yourself and push yourself to be better than you were before to grow you. This is why setting goals is best so you can keep track of where you are. And once you reach those goals set higher goals keep going until you reach the desired level you wish to achieve. Now understand you cannot just set high expectations for yourself if you are at the bottom set small achievable goals that you can build on over time. You have to want to be the best to become the best it does not just happen. Know that in your field everyone is competition and that every day you must strive to be on top because the next person will not lay down for you simply because you are the best. He or she is trying to take your spot so you have to stay on it in order to stay the best. Now I understand that not everybody can be the best at the same time but everyone will not have the same goals in mind for being considered the best. There is always room at the top because not everyone wants to do what it takes to get there. Your top will almost always be different from you competition so don't be afraid to reach for the top and become the best. That is why I say competition is good and that you should aspire to be better mentally so that when you are out there doing whatever it is you will be doing you will know that you give it your all in everything you do.

Remember that your peers will not lie down and let you walk over them, that's not going to happen. Stand up on your own feet and push yourself to be the best. You have to want it for yourself in order that you get the results you are looking for. It is merely up to you how bad do you want it and if you do what are you willing to risk to get it. I can assure you that if you live right and stay in the guild lines you will achieve what you want. It is only hard when you allow it to be. Competition can be hard for you but only if you let it so do your best and the results will show who the better of all is.

You cannot make great business by going at it alone. In the business world you have to have others with you and this maybe a variety of sources. No man has ever gotten things done by doing everything themselves it just does not happen that way. Employ people to be around you that are positive and honest Henry Ford had the work of Thomas Edison among others to help him in his goals. You need good people around you it will help you in the long run. Give credit where it is due show those that you work with that your whole make up revolves around their continued success and let others get their fair share in the pot. Many have made that mistake by becoming greedy and feeling as thou they and only them should get all the credit. Understand it is the people around you that make you who you are and it is because of those people you should contribute your success. Giving back is the key right here with the understanding that those that you have around you in your business are key to your development.

As a member of management I found that if you give your employees credit that it will make them feel good about working for you. Sometimes a simple thank you to your employees can make a world of difference in people. Incentives are great perks in business because it gives them something to shoot for if you have goals that you want to meet. Remember the people around you make the difference in whether or not you succeed or fail. If you're a manager of a company and one day the owners come out and say to you hey you are doing a great job in this department how do you do it simply say that it is the people that you work with that make the difference in how you operate. It is the employees that come in everyday and work hard to keep everything going smooth so sir I cannot take the credit for our success I would have to give it to them. It's that simple lower your pride and give the people around you a little credit from time to time it is not all about you. If you do this I can assure you that the odds will turn in your favor. Use the works of other to help you do not hang yourself out to dry if you can have people there to help you. It is great business when you give others opportunity to do something they love and it helps you gain lasting support for your own success.

Another way you employ people to help you is like this if you have a shoe store do you think you alone can manufacture the shoes ship the product sell the product and everything else that comes with running a store no. if you design them you may have a outside company make them using your design then they may ship them then you may have someone working in your store to sell them to keep up with sales if you have a profitable market and so on and so on. So understand you need people around you and you have to give credit to those around you in order to keep your business balanced. What could be so hard for you to thank the people around you it's not hard at all and once you make it something that you just do it will almost seem automatic for you to thank the people around you that help you to succeed. Practice this and trust that it will excel your business and your results.

Train your mind to know and believe that you control your results and that it is you that can change your outcome. The mind is a sponge and with that being said you should know that a sponge absorbs things. So feel your mind with positive things about you. Change your mind state to help you control your own affairs. This is something in you so it does not to have to be displayed you just have to redirect the mind into know that you have the power to change you, and also the power to control you. This is critical because with this new source of power great thing can come or terrible things can manifest so you have to learn to control the way you think. I know it may sound crazy but if you have been applying the principles you will understand that this holds true that you can change your out come with your thoughts. Believe in your ability to have control and know that it is possible to attain. Your enter strengths can ether move you forwards or it can move you backwards it is up to you to decide.

I have seen people deny themselves this and unknowingly deprive themselves of ever moving ahead. It is that simple so you should trust that you would not do anything that would stop you from achieving your goals. Wait let me rephrase that if you study the principles and have gained the understanding and you truly know what it is you want and that you believe in who you are then you can say you would not stop yourself from achieving your goals. Get the understanding first without it you will only be setting yourself up for failure, and then this knowledge will not benefit you in no way period. You have to know what you want in order to have a control over what you do. This takes some time so don't get discouraged if things do not work out the first time. Just reorganize your plans to fit and keep going towards your goals. Remember it can be controlled and you in time will have the control over it that you desire. Reassurance is okay for yourself it gives you that power needed for the mind to know that you understand and that you have self determination to succeed in anything you set your mind to. I reassure myself daily and keep my mind focused on my goals. My belief is so strong that at times

I unknowingly place myself in better situations for myself it comes without asking it has been manifested into reality without me even seeing. I have a positive mental attitude and with it the laws of the universe align in my favor.

Once you begin to understand that law you to will see the change you seek because it will manifest before you and you will know that you control your own affairs. The mind is powerful and if you train your thoughts to empower yourself then you will begin to open new doors for yourself. Remember it is up to you to change and master the control needed to get where you want to get in your life. Believe in you and others will see you will see the world will see that you truly are the master of your own destiny. Great power comes to those who can motivate themselves mentally to know that they were born to control their outcome in life. It is in you that you make the change in order that you align yourself with law and move yourself towards your goals in life. No one else can do it for you this is something that must start with you for the inside and once you control it from the inside it will then start to show on your outside.

Begin to think of yourself as being on the road to success with endless possibilities, and on that road you travel there are no road blocks you can't handle. A beautiful life lies before you. Know that with whatever you decide to do that success is imminent and it is attainable for you. You can succeed you can have a better life you can live in a world where the odds are in your favor. It is merely up to you to decide whether life will be easy for you or will it be hard for you the option is up to you. Set your goals where you can reach them it will help you to see the change you want over a period of time. You begin to see yourself moving towards your ultimate goals. When faced with a problem don't panic find solutions to fix them learn from them and move on don't waste time away looking at what won't work looking does not solve the problem. Know that you have a goal to reach and reach it. I hear some people say life is hard yea if you make it hard but truth be told how many people sit and think about what makes their life hard. I can tell you this if you have went through this book and have set you goals and are moving towards your goals then you have sat down and looked at the things you have done to make your life hard now you are working to change that for yourself. Life is cause and effect lets say because you walk around not doing the things it takes to succeed the effect is that you never see yourself as a success, or because you never water the plant then the effect would be that the plant dies. People are the same way the cause reflects your effect you have to change the cause to get a better effect plan and simple.

Put yourself in the rocket ship to the top. Know that you can achieve, believe that you will succeed, never put yourself down, and stop worrying about what the disbelievers think remember you control your level of success and it is you that can change the cause to reflect a better effect. Your life is your own script how it ends is up to you. Model yourself after great people in life and study the way they live the blueprint to success has never changed just the things you want in life. It is a proven method that if you apply yourself and believe in yourself and go after what it is you want in life that it can be reached. Your success relies on you how bad do you want it how far can you see yourself going. There are different levels to stop at when the sky is the limit so how far do you plan on going my friends that is up to you. But give yourself the chance to reach your dreams. It is there for you to achieve all you have to do is believe in your ability to succeed and trust that all things are possible. Do not let the negative things that may be around you stop you from achieving your goals. You have to want it so bad that it becomes a desire to you and it burns deep in you that in time you will see that you can have any and everything in life you want but it starts with you believing that you are on that road to success and there are no road blocks that can stop you because you are here to succeed. The ball is in your court and you are the coach the point guard the center the guards you are your own team for yourself. Build yourself up and then you will see you moving towards your ultimate goals in life. Understand that you set the bar for yourself and that it is time that you start to raise that bar so you can get the results that you are striving for out of life. Think that way and watch your life and the things you do start to grow.

Have fun in the business you do because you have to have that laughter to balance the stress that may arise. Feel good about what you do at some point you have to enjoy the work that you are doing. It makes for a better and more productive atmosphere if you can have a humorous side to life. Think about it you are headed to the top so you need to enjoy the times and live life free of boredom. Don't be afraid to smile you owe it to yourself to do so. Make your life enjoyable and love it. I don't want you to get to tied down to all work and no play that is baloney you have to have fun your job should be fun your business should be fun life definitely should be fun that's what makes life great the ability to have fun. Get in the habit of setting aside fun time throughout your day for you to relax and enjoy the breeze. Remember life is all about balance plan your days and keep them balanced.

I hear of so many people that never get any joy out the jobs they have. That is something that I have yet to understand but it is true. You ever go to a restaurant and the waitress has the worst attitude you have ever seen. I mean all you want is to get you order right and get good service and they act as if you told them to screw off or something. Or better yet go to the gas station the attendants can be some of the worst people you can ever meet. And don't let you forget the pump number they get really nasty then. It is sad to say but it is unbelievable how people can hate the jobs they have. I don't understand if your job is so bad then quit and find something that you can enjoy. Be honest with yourself and stop putting yourself through it and please stop putting the people you serve through it. Find things in life that you enjoy doing and if it is a job that you like doing do it. I believe it to be that when you like something that is when you apply yourself more and succeed higher than doing the things you don't necessarily like. So look at those things when looking to change a career or lifestyle. Know what you like and feel good about it I can assure you that it will make it a whole lot easier to add fun to what you are doing. Don't be afraid to let loose and enjoy life from time to time it's healthy to have a sense of humor it is a great stress relief and makes everyone around you feel good to. Do not worry yourself about things remember you control your destiny so control it and have fun.

I use this quote often and it is "love live life" love the things you do live in the moment and know that you make your life. Things happen the way you manifest them so keep a positive mental attitude and enjoy the life you create and stop blaming everyone else for the things that do not go well in your life. Life is what you make it and that is why you should have fun any chance you get. Some people say life is short I believe life is short only when you waste your time complaining and you wake up an then it's to late to enjoy it so start now enjoying the things life has to offer and live and love with passion. These words are true if you live by them and stay true to the things you truly enjoy in life may it be family, friends, your job, a pet or anything that make you feel good inside cherish it and hold it close because those are the things that make you unique and different from everyone else on this plant.

Being rich does not only consist of money alone. True wealth does not come from what you can buy it's from the people that admire you the things you do for others your contributions to the world living a life of understanding and purpose. A balanced life leads to a rich and healthy life hands down. The freedom to live the life you want now that is what being rich is all about. When you find your purpose then you will begin to see yourself becoming rich not on the outside but on the inside and you will understand that is where true riches start. You cannot have money alone and nothing else you will find yourself miserable everyday of your life. Share your fortune with those that are less fortunate give back by showing others of what you contribute your success. No one makes it to the top by themselves. You will see the time come when people enjoy your company you will become well liked by your peers and people will respect the person you have become.

I tell people all the time never burn your bridges with people because you will never know who you may need in the end. You should want to be well liked that is a part of having true riches. Be willing to help others in their time of need remember there was a time when you where in that same spot as well. The ability to help others is a sign of the riches you seek. I am sure by now that you know that this book was not designed to show you a get rich quick scheme no this book is about true riches that you get from a balanced and purposeful life. He that seeks silver will never have enough silver if money becomes their God then that person has a problem. You should not worry about the money it will come just live a purposeful life and enjoy it to the fullest. Once you put your priorities in order then you will begin to see the money you desire but you cannot let the money be first. You can get everything you want in life if you help other people get what they want. Real riches are attainable it's all about how you go about in attaining them.

Never live for money and money alone your wealth will be short lived I can assure you. You have to have something more than money like good health, pleasing personality, a purposeful life, a will to help others, self-discipline, and amongst others a positive mental attitude. Once you have gained these riches you will see your life in a whole new glorious way. Life will become easier for you when you learn how to use the riches you have acquired. You will see yourself rich inside and out, your life will become whole and it will make your life abundant with the fruits of power and achievement. True riches start within never from the outside so if that is what you are searching for start with your inner self and let it manifest unto your outer world. Knowing that you have the power to control your destiny is true riches it is something that is priceless and puts you higher than any mountain peak it is that in which you will see your riches grow. It is that in which you will see life turn for the better. True riches can come to those that strive for being righteous and genuine to all they come across. This is why I must say that to have money and money alone does not constitute true riches and to be rich you must become rich from the inside in order for it to manifest on the outside.

Think of failure as an exit that some take on the expressway of success and you should know that on an expressway you can get off but you also can get right back on. Don't beat yourself up when you fail simply get back on like I said failure is only failure when you accept it as that. No one is perfect so you should expect the best prepare for the worst and capitalize on what comes. Life is filled with many choices it is all about making the best ones for you. You are not going to make all good decision all the time it's what you do with the decisions you make that will make all the difference. When you except failure then you begin to dig a hole for yourself that can be very hard to get out of so let's stay away from that I failed mentality it's not healthy. Do not let your short comings stop you remember you have goals that have a time table so you cannot afford to stop the process because you are hit with a little determent. You should know that failure is also a mind thing and if you do not address it then it will bring you down. You have got to pick yourself back up and move forward it all depends on you.

I have faced adversity on a many of occasions but I never let that stop me. You see I know that if I allow myself to be defeated then I would stand no chance for success. I remember trying to get a job and being turned down over and over. At first I did not understand why I felt that I was a perfect candidate for the jobs I was applying for but still I could never get a break. At times I looked at myself as a failure and because I saw myself as a failure I failed at almost everything I did. Now some may say that my thoughts had nothing to do with that and I would have to say if not that then what. I had defeated myself mentally before I was ever defeated physically. You see you have to win on the inside in order to see yourself as a winner on the outside. With the failure mentality you can expect to see failure almost certain I can assure you. Learn to combat failure with change or as I like to call it possibilities you have to be able to adapt to changes nothings never going to go the way you plan it every time so you have to be ready for that when it comes.

Aren't you tired of making excuses for yourself? If you're not I am for you, you have got to stop hindering yourself from changing your destiny. The fact that poor thinking and the acceptance of failure will keep you from getting closer to your goals should be a sign that you should learn to control it because it is contagious to you as a whole. I also understand that failure can be hard for some to deal with but you have to keep going. We are here only to succeed so failure is not an option. Do not let failure be your end look at it this way you are in the drivers sit where you go is up to you and never forget that. Some people let defeat govern them don't be one of them. In time someone no you have to stand up and not let life push you around learn to push back but harder and demand the results you want in life. It's up to you now come out of your shell and start to run your life. Most people fail because they are not prepared understand failure does not exist where success is present because there is no room for it. No one has to fail but many will fail it's what you do afterwards that will tell the tale. You can do it just believe in yourself and watch what you do in life.

Be honest with everything you do because an honest person is a truly successful person. There is no reason why anyone should be dishonest with their peers. The thing with lying is that you have to remember that lie and it is a total waste of your time when you can just be honest. Nobody likes a dishonest person and that is bad for business so many people now days are dishonest and it has spawned a world wind of distrust in the world. I feel that if people are a little bit more honest with people the world would be a little bit better. You should implement honesty into your character if you are not already honest; believe me it will make you stand out in the world. Don't be afraid to be honest if you think others won't be some people are honest if they see that you are an honest person so don't try to cheat the next person because you are not sure of how honest they maybe. Be the bigger person and practice being honest. Treat those around you fair and the universe will do the rest. Honesty is very important and it will show people that you hold yourself high and proud and they will see that they can trust you.

In whatever industry you work in play by the rules. Be fair and treat everyone in the way that they should be treated. Do not get bent out of shape if you have some that are not team players you will have some of them but you cannot drop down to their level it will only bring you down. Everyone has their own agenda and some people are out to tear everyone else down. If they are miserable they want everyone else to be miserable too you cannot let that effect you if you play by the rules and stick to the plan you can easily get around those types of people. Your life is about you so you shouldn't let others affect you. Besides you are there hopefully because you love your job so do not let others control how you act on your job. Keep your focus on your duties and let the rest be themselves. There is so much going on with the economy and I feel it is because you have so many people now not playing by the rules. One minute they do business this way then they do it the opposite way it's getting confusing you don't know what's wrong or what's right. But if you are honest in what you do I'm sure you want have any problems like that. Just stay honest in your dealings with people and you can't go wrong.

Keep your concentration focused on what you want and you won't go wrong. You have to be able to work around all the things around you and keep your focus. Unless you tell people what your goals are no one will know so you have to look at it as that people don't know your intentions. Do not blow things out of proportion because the people around you do not look at life the way you see it that's not their problem right now you have to stay focused. You have to be honest play by the rules and stay focused in life because there are people out here that get joy out of making other peoples life miserable don't become one of these people and steer yourself away from those types of people. We have to face it that's just the world we live in right now. Maybe it will change some day but until then you have to stay focused. Once this becomes a part of you then you will begin to see that it is almost second nature to you but you have to practice daily and believe in your goals in order for them to be achievable. Honesty is something that I would have to put at the top of the list.

Three things you need are knowledge, desire, and passion for what you are doing. I hold those three things to be true. The knowledge of what you are doing is very important you have to know everything you can about what you are doing in order to be successful. The desire to defy the odds and push through any adversity, and last passion you have to love the things you do in life these are three major things I feel will make you successful in life. You have to have an understanding of what you are doing and that comes in the form of knowledge. Begin to model yourself around the knowledge of what you are doing. Become the master of that field and continue to learn new ways to reinvent yourself daily. It is up to you to learn all that you can and trust that your success depends on how much you know about something. By having the knowledge I can assure you that you will benefit in the long run. Desire can be tricky because not all desire is good so that is something you have to know and control for yourself. Be truthful with your desire and believe in you as a person of integrity and character. The desire to achieve in the things that mean most to you can bring you closer to your goals. Without saying I must say you have to have the desire to get up and change the way you live your life to get the results you seek hands down. Be passionate about whatever you do in life. You have to have passion also in order to succeed it is not just with knowledge and desire that you can achieve but you also need passion for what you believe in.

Part III:

TAKE ACTION AND LIVE LIFE

Now that we have went through the principles and the words of wisdom now it's time to make a serious change in the way you think. These simple exercises will help you do just that. If you do as the text states I can assure you that your thought patterns will change and you will jump start your new and for filling life. It's time to take the gloves off and get down to business. If you are looking for change in your life or a better you then follow along. Once you have got the understanding then you can customize the exercises to fit you.

Did you know that you are the controller of your life? If you did then why is it that you let life control you? You have got to get out of that mode and start taking control of your own life. It's up to you if you want to get the results you want in life. From now on I want you to state to yourself daily that you control your life. Say it loud I would prefer you to say it while looking in a mirror that way you are invoking your thoughts with action and feeling. Believe in the words you speak and know that you can have control over your life. Now I know you are probably thinking to yourself this guy has to be crazy there is no way this will work, but tell yourself this also you have never tried it before and you see the results that you have been getting now what's the harm in just trying something different.

Once you are confident that you control your life you will start to see life totally different. These are positive influences that can jump start you to the change you are looking for. You will feel good and look great. This has to become something that you do daily. You will be surprised at the results that you will get. Start organizing you daily life and try to keep things on a schedule. Things will become much easier when you learn to keep a schedule. Remember you control your life and do not forget it.

In life you can ether live life in cruise control or you can do the steering it's up to you. The decision is yours to make but I suggest that if you want life to be the way you want it to be you need to take the auto pilot off and hop in the cog pit. Start living your own life and change the way you think. I hear of so many people that go their whole life on auto pilot with no desire to make the change, understand you can't just simply say it you have to believe it as well and if you do without me even saying anything you will begin to see your life change for the better. Remember you can have the power to control your status in the world. It is up to you so how bad do you want it. If you have any want for it then go get it the only person stopping you is you. Remember each day stand in a mirror and say to yourself I control my life. You will begin the first step in changing your life for the better.

Opportunity is out there so look for it. Everyday you have a chance to capitalize on opportunities if you can recognize them. Most people go through obstacle after obstacle and for what to get bad results you do not have to be like everybody else. Each day you need to look for the opportunities in life; you know the things that can help you achieve the goals you are setting. Say to yourself I look for opportunities every day and remember to stand in front of a mirror and say it loud with feeling. Now when you go out you will start to look for opportunities for you to achieve. You find new ways to avoid obstacles and not let them stop you from reaching your goals in life. Once it becomes a part of you then you will see that it will become easier to spot opportunities.

Sometimes opportunity presents itself without you even seeing it. It is invisible to the naked eye. Opportunity comes in the form of change and sometimes you know you cannot see change per say but you understand that with change comes the unknown. That's what opportunity is it is change from what you are use to. That is what I believe is the hardest part for people to see when opportunity comes. You cannot be afraid of change if you what to see opportunity there is no other way to see it unless you remove all fear. This century alone is one of the best times to capitalize on opportunities I mean there are so many things you can do to change your life but it starts with you. Remember that the opportunity is there if you can seize the moment and take action. Everyday wake up and say to yourself "I look for opportunities and I will capitalize on them to achieve my goals".

Be passionate about who you are and live inside that and it will show. If you are true to yourself then you will have no problem displaying you to yourself; like I have stated it starts with you and you have to believe in you first before anyone else will believe in who you are first and for most. Mental note to yourself and say this I give to you what I see of myself I am what I am and to that I give you me. The world will only see you in the way you display yourself. So with that being said you know by now that you make the outcome of what you see so why not make it worth wild. It has been called the law of attraction and that means you attract what you get. Train your mind to benefit you and put yourself in position to gain in your lifetime. It is up to you and you have the decision to make it what you want it to be. Never sell yourself short with anything you do give it your all because in the end it will be your defying moment so love what you do.

Life needs action in order to thrive otherwise your life will have no meaning. There is no reason for anyone to live that way period. Off the record I have to speak my mind on this subject because it has been killing me. Some people may think I am awful about this but just take a moment to see it in a different way. This is purely my own belief so it is not to be put with any facts but if I am wrong about it then I can accept that but if I am right then can you accept that to be so.

For starters the government is what I like to call enablers they change the laws spend tax dollars and do exactly what they said they would not do. Every four years we get a candidate for presidency and they say to the people they are for the people we believe that to be so and we elect a president based solely on how we feel. Then in some cases later into their term they start to change the very things that they were elected to do. Honestly how much change have you seen that truly affects the people in bettering us as a nation? We are behind in education, technology, and who knows what else. Walk through your house and see how many of the things in your house we depend on and look at the back of them how many things you think you have in your home that was made in the USA probably none. Isn't that weird but its true sad to say but we have got to do better.

The other day I was pulling up some jobs postings online just in the Memphis area alone 10,000 jobs posted to me that was amazing seeing how everyone I talk to the first thing they say is that the economy is bad and there aren't any jobs out there. The problem is that people are not qualified for the jobs, and instead of people getting qualified they just say there just aren't any jobs out there. When me and my son's mom was still together and she would go out looking for a job we had a system that is fail proof when it comes to getting a job. For one you have to take what you can get before you can get what you want like I said nothing happens over night you have to set goals that are attainable and just start from some point. We keep a folder with the names, addresses, and phone numbers of everywhere she applied. At first she would just go to certain places that she felt fit her I wish that I could tell you that she was always a shoe in when it came to getting any job but I can't. That's when I came up with the solution to her problem we began a campaign to apply to every single job opening that she could apply for. At some points she had applied to as many as 50 openings at a time sounds crazy huh but true and out of that 50 would you believe that maybe ten would have been good possible guaranteed jobs strong statistics but that was true. Think of it this way if she had continued to just apply to what she thought was best for her she probably would have never gotten a job. You have to sell yourself by putting your name out there and establishing a plan of action. Of course she didn't expect to get 50 job offers who could work 50 jobs no all she needed was one. The point I am trying to make here is that there are lots of jobs out there it's about how you go about in getting your name out there to the right people. With that being said I cannot understand why someone would stand and say that there isn't any one hiring when that's just baloney you can't get a job if you never apply.

What does welfare mean to you? If I may let me tell you what I think and it's my opinion so please don't take offense. Over spent control over a persons income that enables them to sit at home and become lazy off the backs of hard working people in America. Let me explain because I know your mouth just dropped to the floor. Not everybody but majority of the people on welfare choose to be plain and simple. I see now more able working young people more than ever before rather than get up and get a job they would rather stand in a line and hope that the system will give them a hand. What happen to the American dream I will tell you this nation is filled with kids and the government has became our parents. We have got to grow up people you know that's what you do when you reach a certain age. This is what I think I don't have a problem with welfare I think the idea of it is great but the abuse of it is what it has become and that is why I am against it. My thing is this if you are trying and maybe that isn't enough then help from the government is good but if you will not even put forth an effort and you would rather sit at home and do nothing that is a problem. There is no reason why any able body person should be sitting at home doing nothing. Then the government thinks raising taxes is the solution no the solution is to stop being an enabler. You can not help any one that does not want to be helped. Let me tell you a story about this system. Now people this had me flipping out my son's mom was not able to afford health insurance for herself my son was covered by my insurance from my job and for her to be insured we would have to be married. She got a case worker to help her get insurance she was working but that just wasn't enough to get insurance for her. Her case worker told her that in order for her to be insured on government assistance she would have to put me on child's support. So that meant for me as a man that takes care of my responsibility I would still have to pay for her to be insured. Notice the key word child's support she is not my child but they where ready to put that responsibility on me and that is funny because I also know of other people that go through that same system and I see boys not men but boys that walk around having babies and they don't have to pay for it but me a man that takes care of mine has to take care of what isn't mine. Don't get me wrong I will and have always done for my son's mother but for me to take on the responsibility of her father's role is just bullshit.

We have got to change how we live and for us as a people to depend solely on government assistance is crazy. It's screwed up and it is because of our inability to do for ourselves. Values have changed and it is becoming apparent that we need the government to survive and that my friend is not the American dream. It should be abolished and people need to get back to working period. One thing we have is a choice to be what we are and the choice to change our outcome the thing is that we have the option to do nothing but complain. That is what a lot of people so stop complaining and change yourself then you will see a difference remember it starts with you. I think the system should be revised and it should cater to the willing to build a better America not the ones sitting at home doing nothing. There are so many people left out because the system is so geared around the so called needy and the people that really make up this country are left to fend for themselves. I don't understand why when a person that is out here trying to do better is turned away but when a person that isn't trying to do anything for themselves or the world get all the assistance that they want. If you know people like this and I'm sure you may know of at least one don't feed into their ideology because it is the very reason why we are where we are. This hasn't just happened this is a domino effect and we will continue to fall if we don't change us. We must take action for what we do and make it count.

Stop saying that rich people have all the money that's even crazier than depending on the government for assistance and then getting mad at the system you are a part of. Rich people don't owe you anything most of them worked hard to get where they are today and those deserve every penny. Now I know you have some that have put a bad name on the wealthy but that cannot be used to judge everyone that is wealthy. What if I said you just can't trust the poor or less fortunate because they are known to steal and be dishonest, you would be offended you would say that some poor people do have a tendency to steal but not you so I cannot put you in a category but you will sit there and place great and decent wealthy people in a category with dishonest wealthy people just because they are rich sounds hypocritical to me don't you think. You are the reason you have not had any change in you life and it will be up to you to make that change. Did you know that there are more self made millionaires today than ever before? You can be one of them but you have to make the decision for yourself. But I also want you to remember that money is not the only thing that constitutes being rich and if you believe that money will make you happy then you are going to have some problems. Do not let money become your God this book is not a how to get rich quick thing it is about finding yourself in order to better your outlook on life and manifest through the mind what you would like out of your life. Listen people it is not the fortunate that has put you in the place that you are in it is merely your own false perception of life. What I would like for you to get out of this book is the know how to transfer your thoughts into reality and to stop blaming everyone else for your problems.

Yes I know how easy it is to do nothing and when a person is trying to do more in life the race gets hard but that is what gives you strength and once you have reached the finish line you will have showed that you are fit to be call great. Some say that the hardest part in changing something is the start process. Yes to commit to change can be hard but you also will go through things throughout the course of your life that can either be discouraging or inspiration that's for you to decide but one thing that is truth is that you must push through in order to see change and the closer you get to where you want to be you will begin to see a change and things will fall to your feet effortlessly. We cannot continue to feed off of the government we have to get back to being a nation where dreams can come true. You see how immigrants come over to the states with a dream and for fill that dream. Their children are better educated because of their will to learn new things. I remember when everybody was upset at Oprah Winfrey when she started building schools in Africa. There are countries that have children that want to go to school and learn. We are here in one of the riches countries in the world and some of our children take these privileges for granted and that is a shame that we have the opportunity to learn and become whatever we want yet our children learn to blame the government for their situations. Stop feeding our children this bull crap and start giving them a chance to be a contributor to society instead of taking from society.

Life is what you make it and until you stop the blame game you will never get out of the rat race. Change is possible but you have to commit to it in order to see it happen. This can be used in anything in life you want if it is something you want there is no reason why you shouldn't be able to get it. As long as it does not affect anyone else then you will not have any problem in getting what you want in life. It is the mind in which things can become a reality you just have to believe from within yourself. Everything in this world started in the form of an idea. Trust you and you will begin to see your life take form. What you do in life is defined by your actions. Live what you talk and believe in who you are that is what you will be judged by hands down. If there is anything in life you should remember it is this that everything you have gotten in life was preformed because of what you wanted or allowed to happen. You have the internal power to change your outcome. I use to use the phrase "life hard" but really life is what you make it. You must be what you wish in order to be what you want period. You have to want more in life to get more in life so change who you are and how you live then you will begin to see the change you are looking for.

Learn to share in your blessing for then you will always have room to receive more when you have given that same gift unto others. Be thankful for what you have and reach for what you would like in life but stay true to you and the people around you. Do not resolve to put people below yourself because everyone on this earth are one in the same we all breath the same air we walk on the same land and we are all created the same. You are no better than the person standing next to you. Learn to love and give and live in harmony with yourself and take control of your own destiny and live life. So many people I see today would rather tear down their neighbor then help bring them up. Now I am a firm believer in the phrase you can't help any one that does not want to be helped but sometimes it takes a person to see from a person that leads by example rather than talk about change. Become a leader in the world and remember like I said there is plenty of room at the top so come join me and the countless others.

Without all the challenges I have had to face in life I do not think I would have been able to convey my thoughts in this way. This book is from mere life lessons and the trials and tribulations that I have went through and seen in my lifetime. Some would say I have out lived my time or I am ahead of my time. I feel that I was blessed to perceive this knowledge in a way to relate it unto the world. Everything that I state is my perception on how to make your life what you want. Trust that if you take from this and apply the principles in everyday life you will see how your life transforms. I cannot go on and say to you that the road gets easier that's just not the case but I can say if you believe in them and trust in yourself then you will begin to take the necessary actions in order to direct your life in the path you wish. You have the control to change your outcome you just have to determine when that time is and when it come what will you do different. I believe also that you should be yourself you cannot pretend because in the end you will find that the only thing that has ever stopped you is yourself. So in order to rise above that you must be true to yourself and give your all in whatever you decide.

I have reached a stage in my life and for you your stage will be different your dreams will be your own you cannot live my dreams or anyone else's you must to have your own. I remember some years back there was this homeless man that hung around the area where I lived. My friends and I would give him clothes, shoes, and money just whatever he needed. One thing about that I never got over was that he never asked us for anything one day we just stared to give him that support our goal was to get him cleaned up and off the streets. He was an alcoholic and he was on drugs and that was common for that area and we saw many just like him all the time but he was more and we felt that if we could give him a boost he could get himself cleaned up. The point I am getting to is that you cannot walk anyone through the door unless he is willing to go through the door. We had good hearts and we wanted to do so much for this stranger who we never really knew but we where blind by that simple fact that he wanted to be there I mean he had a choice and he choose that life style. At that time I never understood why but over time I saw that very fact that it has to be your own choice to change you cannot change for someone else it has to be something that you want for yourself. All the clothes we gave him he sold for more drugs and money we would give him bought his beer his life was paid for by us and he never changed. What would you think do you think that was his plan maybe fate or the learning experience that I have went through and learned from in knowing that you cannot make somebody change if he or she is not ready for that change.

This is what I am saying we all have our own lives to live and we cannot change the next person if they are not willing to change for themselves. Sometimes when you are in a place where you care about someone that becomes a challenge but you have to realize that some of the closet people to you will be the ones that prevent you from every being who you were born to be. "You have to search inside you to find what matters most to you and sometimes what you find is not always what you want", Norris Thomas II.

This is in truth the things that I have talked about over the course of this book. This story comes from a lady that I have become acquainted within the past year or so her name is Ms. Pearl. Ms. Pearl has inspired me in so many ways and I don't want you to think that I have gotten off of the subject at hand because I have not this story is this book and about the trials and tribulations we face in life. She was an only child and both her mother and father have passed she lives alone just her. She has no immediate family and it has made life difficult for her. A few years back she met a man as she would say a great man they both fell in love and soon they were wed. One year later the love of her life passed away and now she is again alone. I tell this story about this woman to give you insight on what the world has become and to open you mind because we can change the outcome of someone else's life, and that with every action we make in life we have to look at who it might effect. We are all one in the same so in some way we are all connected. After she lost her husband things begin to change for Ms. Pearl. Her life became a struggle and everywhere she turned the doors where slammed in her face. When I first met Ms. Pearl we were at the store where I work and we were talking about the ads and how she has a hard time getting out now. I remember her telling me about a ticket she had gotten for parking in a handicap spot and that when she tried to call and get it straighten out because she had her handicap license plate that she kept inside her car because she was instructed that people had been stealing the plates. Ms. Pearl has all her documents showing that she is legally handicap under law but the people that that she talked with had no compassion for our elderly and sent her through hoop after hoop. She has lupus and a lot of other things that prevent her from doing certain things or getting out during the day. When she talks to people to get the matters resolved they make it so difficult for people just like her to get things done, and it is because of the lack of concern people have for anyone other than someone close to them and that is a shame. I sit and look at some of these same people I know would go crazy if someone even thinks to deny someone they knew. Society is off balanced and that is one of the reasons we don't stop to think of who we may be affecting as long as it does not affect them. Now here we have this lady and I know there are many more all over the world just like her that can't get a break because of people's lack of concern. Understand that with every action you take in some way it can either hurt someone or help someone which would you rather do. People always want to put the blame on the way the system is that is baloney because the system was created by someone or some form of a committee so the rules can be bent to assist the elderly. Telling Ms. Pearl that there is nothing you can do about clearing a ticket a simple parking ticket how dare you when she has the proof that shows that she has handicap plates. Instead you want her to come to court and stand downtown for sometimes hours at a time and bring you proof that you already can see with a simple click of a mouse. Excuse me for a minute this subject burns me up and it has everything to do with what this world has became and it is sad and you wonder why the world is in the mess it is in it is because of the selfish, thoughtless, and inconsiderate people that we live with each and every day. This doesn't make any sense but yet it's catered to those that sit at home and do nothing but have babies that they cannot afford to take care of. You give them everything and people like Ms. Pearl or my grandmother who at one point couldn't afford here meds when she had a stroke they have to jump loop after loop. Stop perpetuating the cycle in allowing people to be blood suckers and change the way we value life. Everybody talks about how we are moving forward but that's bullshit because I see it every day our elderly are going through hell and then you tell them that social security is getting scarce and that most once they reach the age of 65 will not have social security well if that's the case why are they still taking it out of the checks of hard working Americans that we pay into but once we get to that age you are telling me that I may not have it. If blessed with the chance to grow old which many have not had that chance but to get that chance to aspire to live that long you will be old one day and think of how you will feel when someone makes life hard for you when you only have the energy to just live that you have to endure such agony to get things done you will be outraged so what do you think the elderly of today feel like. But in this day and time we do not think about that and that is just sad. But once we are faced with that now it becomes a problem and we want to do something about it. We must change the way we live and we have to start with giving our elderly what they desire. Now I am not saying that everybody using the government does not need the government but there are so many loop holes in the system that the ones that really need it do not benefit. Ms. Pearl is one of them and that hurts because her story is just one of many and it's like no one cares or if they do you still have to jump through a hoop to get things done. Now all she has to talk about is why things are the way they are and at times she sees no hope that things will get better for her. I talked with her on another occasion and it was the same and I ask myself why really why is it so hard for someone to be decent enough to see her situation and be understanding. She was telling me of another situation she was faced with and I hate to get in depth with it but I must to give you insight in to what is really going on. She told me of the light company that came in and took her meter and shut her lights off because they said her meter was out dated and that it was not reading right because apparently her bill was too low to be reading accurately. When she tried to get the matter resolved they told her that the bill was not in her name so they could not speak with her. Her father left her the house at his passing and the bill never changed even though they were always paid and never late. They told her that in order for her to get service restored she would have to show proof that her dad had passed. They turned her service back on but gave her thirty days to give proof even though she showed proof they told her she could not keep the service in his name and that she would have to change it over into her name which to get new service that's about 125 dollars plus any other fees. Then she found that the new meter that they placed on her home begin to show her bill 10 times higher than it was before now she is paying more. The bill came out and it was higher even though you could see the major jump in price from the month before verses the month at hand and she was instructed to pay that bill completely before they could do anything. Then she would have to change everything over to her name and for what when she had no problems in over 25 years now it was a problem. So in all she would have to pay the last bill which was outrageous plus a deposit. Now this poor old lady has had to go through all of this and for what to put more money in someone's account. People life cannot be about money that is the problem we are facing. People have put a price on moral values and that makes me sick to my stomach. Everything is about money now and to some that can block the mind from understanding some people's situations.

Let me jump for a minute but understand that all of what I am saying ties in. I feel this system which has put a burden on Ms. Pearl as well as many other elders has come from a repetition of people getting over on the system. Now how can we decipher in the difference and what's hard about doing so. This is where your morals come to part we are all people and as people we cannot rely on a system especially if it hurts our elderly. I understand that there are con artist out here that want to get over on the system but when you begin to lock it down and choose to make it hard for everyone even the ones that need help that is immoral. We must begin to change this inconsistent system that so many in "Corporate America" have so called use to no affect but hurt those that need help. You can change the ways you do business but the crooks are going to always be crooks and they will find new ways to get over.

What I want you to understand is that you have to decide what you are going to do in your life. Will you be a person that makes a difference or just another person in this world? Your greatest asset is your mind young people especially you have so many opportunities that were not available years ago. There are so many way to get to the information you need to succeed that it is just phenomenal. Young people use what you have been blessed with and take action because success does not fall from the sky. Begin to set goals for yourself and mastermind a plan of action. "Your tomorrow depends on what you do today" everything you can imagine can be obtained if you put your mind to it. We are in a state of resistance when it comes to how to use the mind to manifest our desires when it is the mind that gives the solution to all problems and with the mind we can do anything. I want young people to understand that you are truly the future and you have an obligation to the world to be a contributor. I once was a part of that generation when my teachers would tell us that we were the future and it was up to us to decide whether or not we were going to be contributors or not. Just as we had the choice you do as well but remember like I said it's plenty of room at the top come join in don't settle for less because you are worth so much more. I know sometimes you just need some encouragement and that's fine but learn to encourage yourself then encourage others take pride in knowing that you can make a difference in someone else's life. If you take a minute to stop worrying about yourself and give your time to help others you may find that things will begin to change for you. Remember you bring into your life in the order of how you live so how are you living. Treat people in the manner in which you would want to be treated. Some young people have such a lack of respect for someone elder of them and that is just ridiculous. With success come respect and you cannot gain success if you have no respect. So many ask why is life this way for me why, why, why but ask yourself what makes your life. Understand this is about you and your lack of commitment to become a better person. I want you to stop complaining and take action; this is your life and I suggest you start living it. Parents if you raise your children right then they will have no problem in discovering who they are so it is up to you to lay a solid foundation for their success. Allow them to exercise their creative side early because it will show them how to open their creative side of the brain and you need creativity to find your place and use your thoughts to manifest your dreams. Give your children chances by letting them grow and with the right guidance give them inspiration to be whatever they would like in life. Teach them to be respectful and honest not only with the people around them but with themselves as well. Give them hope and show them by example you can't lead a flock if you don't know the direction in which to go. The world lacks role models and today's parents put that responsibility on other people and then when that particular person fells to be a good role model then everyone plays the blame game. That's not the responsibility of someone else to be a role model for your child that's your job and when you child fells then it is your fault not anyone else. It's ok to model someone but your morals can not come from someone that you know nothing about except for their civic involvement. A child can aspire to be a great basketball player like Michael Jordan but he cannot be Michael the man if he has no knowledge of how Michael lives his life. Simply put you get your morals from who you are around hands down. People put so much pressure on celebrities to be role models for their children and I feel it's not their responsibility to do so. You want everybody else to raise your child but you won't raise them yourself. Why is it not your responsibility to be a role model for your child? Why give that to someone else and then get mad when that person turns out to not be what you thought? But if you where the role models in the first place then you would see that there is no one else to blame. Maybe that's it you don't want to be blamed for your child's failure it's easier to blame someone else instead. We have got to get around this and I must say that the principles in this book can get you there if you apply them. Give yourself pride and give your children someone they can see firsthand everyday as a respectable role model.

People this is not rocket science this is simple facts of mind over matter and that when you put your mind to it anything is truly possible. Believe in yourself and stand up for what you believe in. I have three letters for you LLL which stands for Love Live Life and to me it means love the life you have and live the life you where placed here to live. You only get one shot at living life but you have many opportunities to change the course of the life you live. Once you find your purpose and begin to follow that purpose you will see that life truly can be better if you make it better for the people around you. Over the years I was told that my willingness to help change others would go in vain, but today before all that doubted my passion and my purpose in life which some where stuck in their ways so for some there may have been no hope but for me the learning experience I got was priceless. I was motivated to help others in any way I could. I was a voice to some and to others I was hope now let me be the first to say that this book won't help those that are not willing to try it those that are not willing to gain a true understanding of the mind those that burst under pressure I'm sorry but this will not help you. It does not make you less of a person because like I said through the mind all things are possible and if you have chosen to read this in its entirety then you will have the stepping stones to follow in your quest to finding your purpose in life. I went through a lot to get into the state of mind that I am in right now and I have found these principles to be true in balancing your life. You must have a balanced life in order to prosper because life keeps going even when you stop. The only thing is that when you stop your process will stop; you see you can prosper through life or you can let life prosper without you. Understand that life owes you nothing the only person that owes you anything in this world is yourself. It's time to stop the blame game and start taking action everything you have ever done in life was done because you wanted something. So right now what is it that you want. Start thinking of new way to attain them by opening your mind and allowing your brain to do what it was made to do and that is to think and find new way to relay to the outside world your thoughts and plans through the manifestations of your inner thoughts. This is how things have been invented how life has been simplified. Someone had a vision someone had a plan someone never gave up and that is how you have to be you have to have a vision then a plan and then you must go through with it and never give up. Now this is what this book is about your vision your plan and a never give up attitude if you have already gain this from this book then you have what it takes to change your life for the better. Keep a positive mental attitude and you will see life bend over backwards for you.

Take time to soak in the information read it over and over find things in your life to adapt into the principles of this book and change your life. It has changed me and my passion is to share with all my findings and help change the course of someone's life. Give yourself the opportunity to be more than what you have become. For some they may not feel that the mind can be a channel to manifest your desires but for those that believe this is the groundbreaker that could change your life forever. I'm not going to tell you what you should get out of this book that is for you to decide but I will say that you are the maker of your destiny and it is up to you to make your life in accordance to what you stand for. This has no religious barriers it has no ethnic barriers this book is for anyone that has the aspiration to live better and see life for all in a new light.

Get your life in order and go for your dreams. You cannot get anything in life you want if you never try. There is nothing in life that cannot be done. If we can put a man on the moon fly to parts of the world sail the seas and go from where life started then you can do whatever you want. You don't have to be the smartest or the richest person in the world everybody has the same thing that has spawn some of the best creations ever seen and some that have yet to be seen. This friends is the mind and we all have the same it's all about how you exercise it to benefit you. I came from nothing really my parents always told me that I would find what it is that I am here to do and I went through a lot of trials and tribulations to get where I am and I must say everything I went through has trained me for being the person I am today. Nobody is perfect but you can learn from your mistakes and move forward. The problem is that people give up on hope so have faith in you and keep going. Take action and find who you are because the time only sits still when you do nothing about it. Do not let the people around you stop you my friends you have to do it for you and you will see that you will inspire people you never knew you could inspire. I had the inspiration from a true friend and at a time when I was at my low she remained by my side. Funny thing is that after I dropped out of high school we never talked again but I always kept her mentally by my side and because of her I decided to go back to school and graduated 7 years had passed before I ever talked to her again but when I did get that chance I let her know that the memories I had of her kept me going and that maybe without that I may have not gotten to this point. She said to me that she never knew how much of an affect she played in my life. You see you never know who you affect but you must stay true to you and live and stand for something and still to this day when I talk to her I get the same vibe because she never changed who she was and that is what I remembered and I feel that in life to have someone like that is priceless. I could not put a price on that and for that I am grateful to have known a person of her demeanor she is truly an amazing person. A song that she loves which after listening to it has been my soundtrack to how I truly feel about her and as I am finalizing this manuscript I am listening to it and that is "Never Felt This Way" by Brian McKnight. You see people some of the people that are around you if they have a pure heart can give you the inspiration to do what ever you want in life. If you have people like that around you then you truly will see that all things are possible. If you have someone that believes in you then for them don't let them down. I understand that it takes a lot for someone to believe in someone when they have not yet had the chance to believe in themselves. Believe in others and others will believe in you and that is truth you have that responsibility to the people that love you my son is my every breath and when I look at him I ask myself what can I give him at his young age that I didn't have for myself and that would be to show him that all things are truly possible if you believe and if you dream and to give to him what I was blessed to have and that is someone in his corner like I had when everyone else turned there backs he will know that I will always be there just as my friend has been there for me, and I thank her for that because I know that she did not have to but she did. My son's mom has also be an inspiration for me she allowed me to engage in new endeavors and she was always behind me every step of the way she gave me the one gift no one can ever take from her and that is the birth of my son. Through it all I have had so many people that believed in me and to them as I sit at the close of my first chapter in my new journey of life I must pay homage to those that have supported my dreams even when they have been far fetched but always attainable and give to them back a piece of the many things they have given unto me. Everything in this manuscript is me and I only want to give to the world a thought to have a vision and go after what you believe in the choice is yours and you have to make it what you want to get what you want in life. Pass this knowledge to your children and to those around you let it spread with the notion that these are the profound principles of life that through many minds have poured into the mind of one man and expressed through that man with passion and concern for all humanity to live higher than one would ever expect one to live. I am you and you are me you have made me and to the very bottom of the pot to those that feel that all is lost I can say unto you that you can get what you want in life if you believe and live for what you believe in sincerely Norris Thomas II

www.ingramcontent.com/pod-product-compliance
Lightning Source LLC
Chambersburg PA
CBHW021247280526
45784CB00005B/2268